# Teardrops on the Petals
Amanda Justice

Teardrops on the Petals

© 2020 by Amanda Justice

ISBN: 978-1-63110-432-9

All Rights Reserved Under
International and Pan-American Copyright Conventions.
No part of this book may be used or reproduced in any manner whatsoever without written permission except in the case of brief quotations embodied in critical articles or reviews.

Printed in the United States of America by
Graphic Connections Publishing
Chesterfield, Missouri 63005

# Table of Contents

A Few Words to the Poor . . . . . . . . . . . 1
A Peaceful Dream . . . . . . . . . . . . . . 2
A Tragic Anniversary . . . . . . . . . . . . 3
Biography of a Boy . . . . . . . . . . . . . 4
Conversation With Mama . . . . . . . . . . 5
Dependency . . . . . . . . . . . . . . . . . 7
Dollhouse . . . . . . . . . . . . . . . . . . 8
Electronic Candy Consumers . . . . . . . . 9
Happy Loner . . . . . . . . . . . . . . . . 11
Hell . . . . . . . . . . . . . . . . . . . . . 12
I am Your Shadow . . . . . . . . . . . . . 13
In a Field of Roses . . . . . . . . . . . . . 14
Incest . . . . . . . . . . . . . . . . . . . . 16
July Afternoon . . . . . . . . . . . . . . . 18
Kissing the Abyss Goodbye . . . . . . . . . 20
Little Throwaways . . . . . . . . . . . . . 22
Long Distance Lover . . . . . . . . . . . . 30
Love is Fading . . . . . . . . . . . . . . . 32
Memories From a Reflection . . . . . . . . 33
Mini Lighthouse of Comfort . . . . . . . . 34
My Chances Lie Beneath a Grave . . . . . . 36
My Lips are the Colors of a Rainbow . . . . 38
Possession . . . . . . . . . . . . . . . . . . 40
Sadie's Leash . . . . . . . . . . . . . . . . 41
The Blue Rose . . . . . . . . . . . . . . . 43
The Everlasting Rose . . . . . . . . . . . . 44
The Harlot . . . . . . . . . . . . . . . . . 46
The Man of Sublime . . . . . . . . . . . . 47
The Pain Taker . . . . . . . . . . . . . . . 48

## *A Few Words to the Poor*

Tied up in reality's heavy wrath
I come to realize the awful truth,
which is on earth much is taken
away and the value one discovers
is implacable.

Not much I have become and
maybe that was intended but the
hopes I once put on this world along
with its dreams has vanished.

Almost always in lonely times
the world has let me know where
I'm bounded to be in poverty and
without answers.

The worst I can say is the stress
playing its role day in and day out
with very little relief but when this
relief comes I think of you and pray
that through Godspeed He will take
me to you.

Every hour in despair is worth
every moment we once shared.

While awake the dwelling on earth
may rip every last shred of joy in
me but when I finally do close my
eyes and never wake up let the whole
world know this dream is not wreckable
for when I reach and touch heaven's
gate all my wealth will return with
a higher value.

## *A Peaceful Dream*

Compassion is not hate
nor is it's nature deceivable.
It is opening one's eyes and becoming perceivable
to one and everyone's unpredictable fate.

Everyone is unique, radiating with a special gift
that gives hope to a dim room with more delight
then just this world of gloom but this giving comes
from the heart making bad things drift.

Coming together is a wonderful feeling
allowing each gift to shine bright
creating with beauty an amazing sight
with words said from a peaceful saying.

What kind of leader would it be
to initiate such actions with so many giving
guidance to those who have, yet, no penny bringing
back faith for a brighter tomorrow to see.

Grudge, lies, and despair forever fade away
filling this world with unbreakable love
that makes each spirit freely move
with gentle words that many will say.

A wonderful dream coming true
for so long, we will finally know
what real beauty there is to show
looking beyond with knowledge and a clue.

# *A Tragic Anniversary*

Long, long ago on this very same day
I lost my everything in a tragic accident.
Off, to a fancy profession far away
the horrific news brought such lament.

I finally found love for the first time
in the eyes of someone so dear to me but the
loss, so great, it seems I have committed a crime
and all is heart broke that I can see.

Oh, how I should have remain
and maybe this event would not have been
wondering as I look out my window into the rain
but the day before, I would never have seen

What loss really is and how it feels
to deal with it, letting hurt grow
while leaving a scar that never heals
making the days pass so slow.

Memories might feel your place now but,
I believe a precious dream will come to be
in paradise where beauty is to show
and upon you, my eyes will see.

## *Biography of a Boy*

Despite his mother was neglectful and said "Goodbye!"
He often thought of her existence and alone in
a bedroom he would often cry.

Father, well occasionally, in his own way
planted fear and resentment in his son's heart but on most days,
the boy and his father exchanged very few words and had little to say.

Growing into awkward youth
being big, yet shy and internally fragile like a wallflower
the insults of his peers added to his sorrow without anyone's help to soothe.

They bluntly announced he was ugly making the boy's esteem sink below dirt
causing the razor marks on his wrists to drip a crimson waterfall whenever he
peered at his bathroom mirror and saw his own wretched reflection gazing back.
Still he would go back the next day while trying to cover up his black pit of hurt.

Beyond the words, money was gold
and what little he possessed
their friendships, oh surely some sold

All the while, in the shadows, solitude was near
and finally he lost his small possessions then his greedy friends
and once again all that remained was loneliness his biggest fear.

One breezy morning during the fall
he bravely took the gun from the cabinet
and decided to ease the pain by ending them all.

# *Conversation With Mama*

Remember when it was you and me in that small simple apartment many years ago when life seemed less complicated and the dangers of the world did not cross the threshold of my little innocent mind. I felt safe and guarded under your protective wing, even though we lived in the heart of a high crime area in a big city that was notorious for being rampant with violence. Despite our surroundings, we were barricaded in that small simple apartment like a mama bear and her baby cub. In those days, when I was just a cub, there was hope and joy in your eyes, even though luxury and abundant riches were not a part of our daily routine. We were comfortable and content with the daily things that most people with abundant riches took for granted. Our strong attachment along with the hope and joy in your eyes was all I needed at that precious time. Indeed it was a very innocent time of close bonding between a mother and her child. Eventually our strong bond began to break as soon as the years went by and I grew up. The joy that was once in your eyes turned to sorrow and thunderstorms that precipitated down your pale cheeks. Instead of remaining the sweet adorable daughter, I blossomed into an unruly disobedient teen. Along with my soiled reputation that brought those thunderstorms to your dark eyes, the lack of financial stability did not help to alleviate the storms erupting so frequently down your worried face. In the beginning, we were at least able to enjoy the simple necessities of clothes, food, and a modest roof over our heads. On the contrary, as the years passed and the cost of living went way above your income, our peaceful happy connection was strained and became catastrophic. I went from a child who really appreciated you to an ungrateful, sarcastic, teen who enjoyed the thrill of rebelling and became a sore to your eye. I wanted the luxuries that everybody else seemed to have, without realizing that you also would like to have them too, but never once did you ever turn your back on me and resent me for the material things you always managed to do without. Instead you would always give me advice to stay clear of danger such as a broken heart, teen pregnancies, and being someone's puppet for anything. Did I really take your wise words with me mama when I was a curious wild youth? You already know that I did not, and my misjudgments have living proof that destroy my false alibi. Since I was sixteen, I have been raising your grandson and now I know what it is like to be a single mother without any connection from the father. This education in the real world, has opened my eyes to appreciate all the hard work you put into raising me without the help from the man that you pointed out was my father. I am so sorry Mama that it took me so long to finally give you my apology that was way overdue for all the sacrifices that you made and how I undermined them before. Just as those thunderstorms in your eyes, I feel that those same thunderstorms are about to fall down my cheeks as I now stand over your grave and find it so difficult to say goodbye. My hands tremble as I place this basket of beautiful pink roses upon where you rest. I pray that there are pink roses in heaven, because I know you really adored them and I hope that one day I will be with you in that rose garden when they lay me to rest.

# *Dependency*

Receiving his glass of champagne with ebullience
he gives a decent tip to the tapster and after many rounds
slowly fades his alcohol tolerance along with his financial allowance.

Constant intoxication drawing him away from a dream.
Too much stress is to blame.
Why these goals of his not what they seem?

Goals of longing and power,
an imagination filled with utopian thoughts
like achievement in climbing up the success tower.

But images as these last for so long
and the time to make such things real can be
difficult, making it seem in reality dreams don't belong.

Tantalizing as life can be
his habit represses his fears
putting him in a state that is care-free.

Eventually the reality of making dreams come true
will demolish if there is no stop to the bottle but sadly
his dreams have evaporated and to the bottle he will relinquish.

## *Dollhouse*

One Christmas when I was a child
my parents bought me a dollhouse.
In fact they draped a red blanket
over the house because it was
too big for wrapping paper.
Besides my dolls, toy furniture
began to accumulate inside this house.
Looking back, I recall that the
furniture was mainly yellow and gray.
These colors matched the house
and two toy vehicles that
were placed right outside the house.
Taking pride in my possessions
I cleaned the house when
the dust would collect.
Unforunately, now I am no longer a child
but one miserable adult who dreams about the past.
Ironically, I had more success and
possessions at eight than twenty-eight.
For that dollhouse I received on Christmas
will be the last house I ever see.
Where in the hell is my dreamhouse along with
the flashy, updated vehicles that I
can show off to family and friends?
Oh I somehow forgot
a person can not thrive on a
small income of scrubbing filth
and waiting tables to gain the luxuries
we were so promised as children.
Even bursting sweat and tears to achieve our goals does not
guarantee all the prestige and possessions when you are an adult.
For this is why I do not want to grow up
but remain a child in fantasy land.

## *Electronic Candy Consumers*

I have been a world traveler for about
two years now without the use of a plane,
a cruise, or even a train.

All I had to do was post a few sexy,
glamorous selfies that just screams
I am on the market and ready for a
good time along with a few details
mostly false, but a couple true of my
enchanting personality and wonderful life.

Now the enchanting and wonderful part
is definitely false, but with a few electronic
lies and the only God given blessings I
received which is a voluptuous set of
breasts that reveal a pale white cleavage
just makes the gentleman callers come one
by one with drooling tongues despite the
fact that I live in a slumlord's shack and
bust my pretty little ass at some odd
job that I will soon exchange for another.

I am the same way with my sexual encounters
as I am with all the jobs I had in the past, most
think they seen sightings of an alien because
my appearance to each of them is very few
I do not keep in touch with many of these
encounters, the longest I have held onto a
lover's telephone number was a month.

Maybe to some of you who are a part of
that old school mentality might think this
is shameful and aimless.

However, like traveling state to state or
going to different continents around the globe
people, especially lovers are the same way.

You can not have too many for there are
so many flavors of candy as well as the
many appetites of sex.

I have friendly acquaintances from all over
the world to Africa then Europe and back to Asia
but of course let me not forget the kinky Texan
cowboy who took me for a roll in his haystack last night.
When I think of all the fun that is out there
I really do think it is time for me to switch
the current work line of waiting tables to
fulfilling the desires of all my electronic
candy consumers.

## *Happy Loner*

So many are so certain that the company
of others brings satisfaction and sunshine
to the lonely, sole existence of just one.

They even insist that one cannot be fully
whole unless there is a companion to accompany
all the joy and rough patches of the journey.

However with each painstaking day that drags by
I have discovered that humans do not ease the rough
patches but are the ones who cause the stumbling blocks.

One does not have to conduct an arduous study to see
how some inventions and thought patterns of work, paranoia,
prejudice, and dominance have made humans a nuisance.

A once good spouse who has dropped and replaced you for another
deemed to be more entertaining, a fellow employee who needs to prove
self-worth without grasping the concept to mind one's own damn business.

On the playground or hell anywhere for that matter
the in crowd who wants to bully the misfits,
an old friend who abandons you for the in crowd
The tight ass snob who keeps getting rich when a poor fool takes
all the workload and lands in the cold, because some other greedy
monster keeps raising the cost just to be a member on this planet
that translates into the Universe's Ball of Miserable Rejects.

Space shuttle please carry me up and away so that I may become the
sole Earthling among the crimson creatures of Mars, the caramel rock aliens of
Venus , the Saturn Ringlets, or even the blue fluffy figures of Neptune

And after my arrival, let all the miserable, pathetic, annoying, problem
causing Earthlings fry when the Universe's Ball of Miserable
Rejects collide and crash with the scorching rage of the sun.

## *Hell*

A great despair has
come across me.

I walk alone in
shadows of horror
without hope or plea.

Make believe is all I do
for I am tired of this scorching pit
that has no ending, but lingers
like a nightmare and the devil
refuses to let me wake up.

Oh how that special angel came along to wipe those
sorrowful tears, but in the end there was love no
more so now my angel is nowhere near
for she flew the coop and is now above
and every day I am tortured with her memory
down here in this endless heat.

## *I am Your Shadow*

When you walk along a sandy warm beach
I walk along the same wet sands
because I am your shadow.
When you wrap your strong arms around my back
I am encircling your big frame with my limbs
because I am your shadow.
When you wet my cheeks with your kiss
I will drench your entire face with my tongue
because I am your shadow.
When you collect a bouquet of my favorite flowers for Valentines
I will gather your beloved chocolate candy for Lovers' Day
because I am your shadow.
When you promised forever to uphold your vows
I still have remained forever and true
because I am your shadow.
When you stab my soul with insults
I will douche your feelings with gasoline and set to fire
because I am your shadow.
When you slam, my once flawless face, into a boiling skillet
I will push your entire body into the steaming hot oven
because I am your shadow.
When you crack my skull with your power punch
I will grab a chainsaw and separate your head from your entire body
because I am your shadow.
When you pull my hair with a sharp razor to my throat
I will shave your entire head then tattoo profanity while you are sleeping
because I am your shadow.
Finally, when your anger melts into a long anticipated apology
I will be there to accept, despite the previous atrocities
because I will forever remain your devout shadow.

## *In a Field of Roses*

My head tilted gently up
when I heard this familiar voice
call my name to follow in rejoice.

When I got to my feet
I realized this was no ordinary place
and all was harmony that shown before my face.

A beautiful man smiled as he gently locked his hand in mine
and led me around the floral field.
My worldly existence seemed to vanish into this dreamscape he revealed.

The atmosphere was lit up
bringing forth the golden highlight
of his hair and eyes radiating so bright.

We came by a chapel garnished with marble
inside we went and so many appeared
while in my heart the Gospel neared.

After the priest spoke the last word,
all joined in to sing and give grace
when I spotted my Grandfather's face.

He was a few rows to the back
standing in praise, raising his voice with all his might.
It gave me peace to see such a sight.

Everyone seemed so well,
everyone was at peace
no one had knowledge that they were decease.

Sanguine was in the air
as we left the towering feature
just to be a part of the delightful picture.

In me, the burdens I dealt with before
I experienced this carefree state
were no longer, for this was a new fate.

A fate which would one day be. Until then sorrow
will remain but I will walk in a beautiful paradise
and despite death I will have so much to gain.

## *Incest*

Oh father, you are most wise than any other man that has crossed my threshold of admiration and I think you will always remain the special someone who shares with me the incredible delights that help each other remove our troubled thoughts away by washing these dreadful, worrisome toils of stress and temporary escape into our secret world of forbidden pleasure.

We have explored pleasure in different rooms of the family house.

We have also had secret ventures in your orange automobile that was parked beneath a canopy of trees in the cool evenings.

These trees and the darkness of the night helped us cover up our dirty, but exciting secret from the finger pointing, unbreakable stares, and gossip that most ordinary people would not understand, because father you and I are not like those ordinary people, rather we are anything but ordinary, because we challenge what others choose to describe as eccentric and for that we are not ordinary but brave to experience the love that blossoms between two lovers even though I call you "father" and you call me "sweet daughter."

Despite the fact that we do not have the same blood pulsating like a tidal through our veins, even though your age is many oceans away from mine, your wisdom and love is more powerful than the stranger who donated sperm for my creation and left me on the doorstep of despair.

Even though despair opened its door wide, I
now have discovered a paternal figure in you
my friend, my lover, my husband, my everything
and as an honor I shout out "father" preferring
this over the others, even when we are alone amongst
the exotic sensations of outer space and your desired
rocket reaches its peak and explodes inside the walls
of my pink cave that is when you reply back and say
"I love you my sweet daughter."

## *July Afternoon*

Just like spring water clarity describes
my memory of that warm July afternoon
when my eyes laid upon him.

Toiling with laborious routine
he came and brought me out
and gave me such a delight.

Bright eyes glowing with zest,
a smile so rare that is smooth
and modest, a faint dimple
within his chin.

Comparable to the face
that of a beautiful angel
oh how he radiated among
the ordinary.

Maybe for this reason I ached with desire to
reach out and touch the creation that
stood before me and his vast knowledge
of so many years dwelling upon this earth.

A foreign tongue that was calm
and soft oh how I wanted to taste
the fruit of this exotic creature.

Of course him and I knew
the tragedy of the division
in our ages.

However, among the rest of my
fellow youth none did bring me
such desire as did his age with
its wisdom.

Oh how I prayed that temptation
would fail to unfold and pure in
action I had hoped to remain

but temptation did get its way
when I handed over my innocence
and shared a sinful bed during that
hot July afternoon.

# Kissing the Abyss Goodbye

On so many nights you cry wanting
to kiss the abyss goodbye.

Goodbye in letting go of past monsters
who will forever stay locked up and
forgotten.

Here all the angels that you thought
would stay lied and grew apart finally
they went away.

Some of them were once your family
and friends, but suddenly they betrayed
you causing the good times to end and
the selfish beasts to emerge.

After you realized this horror, any
remaining desire was destroyed leaving
a spirit to suffocate.

Ignored now for so long, attention evaporated
from those creatures you use to be among causing
a heart to crack from being filled with tears.
"What have I done for the decision
of those far gone?" you ponder while
staring at the infrequently used phone
that now belongs to you.

With only courage left and a truthful
companion, the music your gift you
swing back the last drop of alcohol
drowning away second guesses of leaving
then realizing, "Maybe freedom was here
with me all this time and I may leave the
torment miles below."

If you ever get coroneted and fame
becomes your friend let the past demons
be forever lost without summoning them
at any cost.

For you are kissing the abyss and
its monsters goodbye and with all
hope, you won't be back.

# Little Throwaways

As the snow came down and sprinkled the roof of the small, yellow frame house which stood in the heart of nowhere with more trees than buildings, Eliza was giving birth to her second child, Princess. Luck be it for this coming child, the father promised to be the solo financial benefactor. However, about five years ago prior to Princess, Eliza gave birth to her first child, Daniel. Now unlike Princess, baby Daniel was not so fortunate because his daddy was always absent and hardly ever dependable with money. If that no account ever did maintain a job for at the most a couple months the earnings would benefit the neediest and cheapest hooker. Usually some middle age woman who looked like a wretched train wreck with a few teeth missing and a heavy made up face which consisted of bright blue eye shadow and pink powered blush caked onto the whore's fat cheeks and top it off with frizzled bleached hair. Besides pumping money into some local used up wreck, he would get wasted at the dingy waterhole in the nearest town a few miles down the road. Because of the lack of financial stability with his father, Eliza disregarded Daniel onto her parents while also giving up her claim and responsibility of the child. In Eliza's state of mind she did not have to care for her own child if she could not reap the benefits of the father's income.

Up until the age of ten Daniel thrived in his grandparent's love. They doted on this boy until a car crash took them both away. Instead of the familiar warmth and kindness he received for ten years, his existence now became isolation and bleak as an orphan among the many other orphans. No one reminded him how special he was, but soon others felt the timid nature reeking from Daniel and so to feel better about themselves they would humiliate and physically assault Daniel if not on a daily basis then at least every other day. About a few weeks after arriving at the orphanage, Daniel had an encounter with Robbie. Robbie was thirteen years old and much taller than the children his age. Robbie and his buddies at first made statements to Daniel such as " Your mom and dad did not want you because your such an ugly pain in the ass and they were to embarrassed that a loser like you came from them. " Eventually the abashing comments turned into punches and head diving in the most soiled and dirty toilet bowl.

This torment continued until Daniel left the orphanage as soon as he turned eighteen. Daniel had no sense of direction or concern on where his life would be going. He roamed aimlessly for many years around the country, from state to state hitchhiking and hopping freight trains in filthy, ragged clothes. Along with this vagabond lifestyle, Daniel carried boiling animosity toward happy families that seemed to cross his field of vision quite a bit. His existence was already hard enough, but images of strangers admiring and showing devotion to their children just really rubbed it in Daniel's face what he did without while growing up in that horrendous orphanage. As cliche' as it turns out Daniel dealt with his solitude and frustration with alcohol he purchased through spare change given by strangers. When the spare change ran out and reality kicked in Daniel was consumed with heavy sorrow. One cold, frosty December morning before Christmas Daniel realized he was too broken to continue through this wretched wilderness people call life. So instead of hopping on the nearest train, he walked right in front of it.

Contrary to the unfortunate life of Daniel, Eliza cherished the arrival of her newborn baby girl. From the very first time Eliza laid eyes upon the infant, she immediately wanted to protect it from the harmful world. Besides the usual checkups from the doctors, Eliza would make extra visits to the hospital in order to relieve her incessant fear that Princess might be inflicted with a new disease. If there was such small things as a cough or minor cut Eliza would run Princess to the emergency room. The doctors and Princess's father tried to comfort Eliza by saying " You need to calm down. This is neither healthy for you nor the child." However, when Princess reached the age where she had to attend school, Eliza's fear escalated. The father not only went up to the elementary school to enroll his daughter, but he also had the workload of trying to convince his wife that Princess would not be harmed by other children who attended the school. This tedious discussion went on for weeks with his overbearing wife.

When the day arrived for Princess to share her existence with other children and those hours without the shackles of her mother, well that day did not go so great. That morning the father had another heated argument with Eliza, which he already anticipated with dread. On top of that, immediately when Princess entered the three story, red brick building she became very timid and almost unanimated like a statue. She spoke very little and mainly kept to herself. During social time, such as lunch and recess, with other children did not seem to cure Princess from her shyness, but instead made it worse. She would set at a small table away from the other group of youngsters and if they occasionally said hello she would nod her head and immediately look down. This went on for a few days and her teacher became concerned when some of the other students began to poke fun of Princess. After the teacher had a conference with Eliza and the father, there was a big blow up when they got home " This is all your fault! All those times running to the doctors for unnecessary purposes Eliza! Look what you did to our daughter! Now she is so fearful of the world she cannot make friends or learn. " Eliza stormed in " Damn you, it's not how I brought my daughter up you bastard it's those brats that are intimidating our daughter! I knew this was going to happen!"

After going round after round of endless arguments, Princess's father succumb to Eliza's demands and removed Princess from the school. He promised her school teacher that Princess would get a good education in another school and that she would see a therapist. However, those became broken promises when Princess was almost hit by an oncoming truck. Eliza was inside cooking dinner while Princess wondered out and into the street chasing her pet hamster, Toby. By accident he got free from his cage and ran out. A few seconds after following Toby into the street a truck was nearing just about eight inches away from the girl when Eliza happened to look out her window and see the heart pounding site of her daughter soon to be hit. Immediately Eliza screamed as loud as she could " Princess get out of the street!" The girl immediately recoiled back from the street and into her mother's arms. Eliza's heart was pumping as if she was in a race for what seemed like ten minutes after. She had trouble catching her breathe and nearly passed out. Even though she was always fearful of her daughter's well being, she never had that caliber of fear rush over her all of a sudden like a dreaded tidal wave and she certainly did not want to experience that ever again. Since the basement was big enough for bookshelves and numerous toys, Eliza decided that it would make a perfect area for giving lessons to Princess as well as her bedroom. Besides that, Eliza also realized that it would be impossible for Princess to wonder off and away from home simply because the basement did not have windows. Eliza also planned to readjust the basement door so that it could only be locked from the outside of the basement. This deep tucked away space had the same purpose as a box. In Eliza's eyes Princess was a rare, expensive, porcelain doll that was too precious for the reckless world above to break. For many years Princess thrived in that basement. Her only company was her father and Eliza. Eliza would frequently descend the steps to deliver a lesson plan for Princess, feed her, bring her upstairs to bath ,but would immediately bring her back down the basement. If Eliza or her husband wanted to spend quality time with their daughter they would descend into the basement. Besides her parents, the only other company she had to the outside world was books. Eliza limited what material Princess could read for she did not want her daughter to be corrupt by vulgarity and violence. What Eliza allowed was childish elementary fiction books with a ton of pictures even when Princess grows into late adolescence.

    Many years had passed and there was no break from this innocent, monotonous dwelling for Princess until she turned eighteen. Her father's health was slowly deteriorating and at times he could not even get out of bed. Less and less did she see her father. Eliza faced the dreaded truth that her husband had to be hospitalized. She was so exhausted from the many trips to see him and the enormous stress that would result from his death. Eliza truly loved her devoted husband and his passing would not only burden her emotionally but financially as well. Even though Eliza never did live extravagantly with an unlimited amount of jewelry, a mansion, or lavish trips around the world, she did reap the simply modest necessities in life. Without her husband and provider, Eliza and Princess would not even be about to enjoy the simple necessities. On one cold December afternoon this tragic loss came true. A few weeks after his passing, Eliza would daily go apply for work. The only offer she got was a part-time minimum wage job waiting tables. She even tried to cut down on her spending, but that did not solve the problem. The rent for living in the small, yellow frame house was due and Eliza began having pounding headaches along with panic attacks on how to stop herself and Princess from living in the streets.

    Eliza racked her brain for solutions until she came up with something that could possibly make money, but also be a forbidden sin. Eliza glanced at her reflection in the mirror and realized that she had accumulated wrinkles through the years. Her youth was lost and could not be recovered. An old lady was staring back at her. However Princess was blooming into a beautiful young lady. Men will adore her, like they once did Eliza. With this adoration money could grow for the two of them. So the next day and with a couple hours before the first male guest arrived with his hard earned cash, Eliza prepared Princess on how to be a woman and satisfy a man. When the doorbell rang Eliza's heart started beating. After he handed her four hundred dollars, Eliza led the tall, slender, middle age, Caucasian down the steps toward her scantily dressed daughter. As soon as Eliza ascended the steps and shut the basement door she ran into her bedroom and placed a pillow above her ears so she could not hear what was going on between Princess and the stranger. Tears began to fall down Eliza's face. This was the first time Eliza ever disregarded her daughter so cheap and it was painful for her to do so. It felt like she was pawning a very precious family heirloom.

Despite the emotional rollercoaster of breaking into this forbidden routine, by the eighth week Eliza's guilt completely vanished. She could not believe the thousands upon thousands of dollars this deed brought to her wallet each month. She was a great distance from poverty. Monetary overflowed in greater amounts now than ever before when her husband was the provider. In the beginning when Eliza had guilt she would take the money and buy Princess gifts. Princess never would request her mother to make extravagant purchases even with the enormous amount of money she earned. Basic necessities such as food, clothing, and new copies of her old rugged books. Eliza would also buy fresh bed sheets and covers for her daughter. Somehow the guilt ridden mother completely changed on Princess. Little by little when Princess would make a small request Eliza would complain " I bought that for you not too long ago. How much more do you need? " Eventually her responses turned to scoldings. For example, when the weather got cold and Princess was down to her last blanket that not only had many holes, but was also soiled from sweat, saliva, and semen she kindly asked her mother for a new one which Eliza shouted " You are such a fucking needy brat! Go to your bed and cover your face with the blanket. Oh and by the way, stay the hell out of my sight!" Princess did not put up a fight, but walked away teary eyed.

Besides her mother, eventually some of the more disturbed customers began to use Princess for their bizarre pleasures. A heavy set man with a southern accent always showed up at different times on Thursdays. Princess knew when he was in the house because she began to recognize that eerie pattern of whistling. Even though she was in the basement, the whistling permeated throughout the entire house. Immediately, when she heard his noise, Princess became alarmed. Next he would enter the basement switching off all the lights as he descended the very last step. The spacious room would be pitch black for about five minutes. Then the room would get a bit brighter when the stranger finally turned on his red flashlight. After the sudden interruption of dim scarlet light, Princess got even more scared by the sight of him staring directly at her as her rocked back and forth in a sturdy wooden chair. He would not say anything, just stare and rock for what seemed fifteen minutes. In addition to the watchful eyes of this mad man, Princess was chained to her bed. On previous occasions she had tried to escape the weird company her mother forced upon her. Besides the basement door being locked and chained like a prisoner to her bed, there was no escape. Yet with all of this, Princess endured much more torment. When he rose from the chair and removed what little clothing Princess wore, he began to light a cigarette. He took one puff and then placed the heat onto her delicate skin. She tossed and turned while screaming for her mother. Instead of coming to her daughters rescue, Eliza recounted eight hundred dollars he paid as she thought of different ways to spend it on herself. After the man left, Princess spent the entire lonely night whimpering in the dark.

    When morning came Eliza went to the basement with the intent of preparing her daughter for the afternoon clientele. These customers tended to be drenched with sweat and odor consequently from the early morning hours of hard labor. After Eliza unlocked and removed the chains, she yanked her emaciated daughter out of bed. As she did this Princess began to weep. " What the hell is wrong?" Eliza snapped. "Momma I am tired of that weird man hurting me. Look what he keeps doing to me." Princess immediately lifted her translucent gown to display multiple red patches along her torso. Eliza rolled her eyes and shook her head " So I guess you want sympathy because your name is Princess. I don't know why I even gave you that name because you are not royalty, but only a filthy little used up whore. No man with high ranks will ever want to marry you for they know you are no more than a dirty tramp that everyone has had a turn with." As a result, Princess did not say anymore but wish for her own life to end.

    Besides those dreadful visits from the sadistic smoker on Thursdays, Princess had to endure another client's twisted fantasy. This time he was tall with severe acne scars and a protruding Adam's apple. Also he was afflicted with a bad case of nearsightedness that was immediately noticeable due to his thick glasses. Not to mention his buck teeth were far from being a pearly white smile but instead very yellow and cracked. Most of the customers were average looking and nothing to brag about when it came to physical appearances. However this particular one rated very low on the attractive scale. Princess assumed that he paid to lash out at her as a result of all the teasing and rejection he went through for being ugly. His sessions with Princess started off with a couple Saturdays a month then he began to come more often. These meetings were therapeutic to his low self-esteem. They did more for him than those tedious visits to the psychologist. His very first time with Princess consisted of spankings. The chains around her arms were unleashed so he could maneuver her body over his knees in the traditional spanking position. She dangled as he consistently smacked the bare buttocks. With each spanking, the blows kept getting more painful. Consequently his powerful force left the flesh black and blue. However, this stranger's cruelty did not seize. As a matter of fact the spankings turned into something worse. He began to punch and kick her. If physical abuse was not enough, he would also shout profanity, " I can do whatever the hell I want to do, you are my little bitch and there is no escape!" This monster was correct because Princess could not escape due to the restraints that forced her to be held captive in the bed.

While it may be true that Princess was under Eliza's thumb and these wicked men, finally freedom did come her way. The key to freedom happened to be sharp scissors. Eliza noticed that her daughter's hair was getting too long and it constantly had tangles. Therefore one morning before the customers started to flood in, Eliza descended the basement to cut the long golden locks. She quickly removed the shackles and chains then pulled Princess from the bed. Despite the fact of having many bruises and feeling very weak, Princess's frail body struggled with Eliza over the razor sharp scissors. At last Princess gained power over the scissors. They were in her delicate pale hands. Immediately, she pointed the sharp end of the scissors toward Eliza as if they were a potential weapon of threat. Silence took over for a few seconds while Eliza stared at her daughter in shock. Soon the silence broke when Princess said " I don't want to hurt you even though so many times you have stabbed me in the back. You have made profit off my pain. When father died we could have stuck together as a team, but instead you sold me like a piece of unwanted trash!" Tears began to roll down Princess's face as she continued, "Those cigarette burns and beatings really hurt, but when I think long and hard about it your betrayal will forever haunt me! You didn't even help me when I was down in that dirty basement screaming for you!" Princess paused a minute and wiped the falling tears and to catch her breath then began again " I still do not want revenge for all the horrible shit you allowed to happen to me. All I want to do is leave without a struggle from you. You will have to find some other way to get money, because I am not going to be your meal ticket anymore!" Suddenly Eliza knocked Princess down and began to choke her. With the scissors still in her hands, Princess started swinging her arms at Eliza. Finally the scissors went into Eliza's left eye. Blood sprinkled down the left side of her face. Shaking, Princess ascended up the basement steps. When she heard the bloodcurdling screams coming from the basement, she looked around the house for something to make it stop. Princess looked not because she was afraid someone else would hear, but because she could not stand to hear that her mother was in excruciating pain. As a result of continually looking, Princess found the pistol in Eliza's bedroom drawer along with a good size amount of money that once again was a painful reminder that her own dear mother profited from her own torment. Once more tears began to spill from the young girl's eyes. She descended into the basement. Before she fired the gun at her mother, Princess said " I am sorry." Immediately the screams stopped and Princess was standing alone in silence. A minute later Princess put the gun to her own head and fired.

## *Long Distance Lover*

Oh how I lost count of the many times I cried
out to the heavens, and asked the Maker of
all creations on earth "Oh why would He place
the one I adore so far to my reach
while I am teased by my glances of lovers
who are near and in one place?"

Oh how they do not suffer
the insatiable thirst for the phantom lover
that is many miles, many seas, many
lands away from their home.

One does not know true
love until they traveled those many miles,
many seas, and those many exotic lands for the
sole purpose to release one's mind from the
torture of forever being more than a long distance
call from the handsome phantom that thrives within
these precious short calls that we put all
our time and devotion so hard into each day.

However, our routines do fill with worrisome toils
that can often divide the joyous intimate
hours I have with my phantom lover into a few
days apart, and the man, woman, or child who
came up with the phrase pertaining to distance
making the heart grow fonder, well those long,
cold days apart makes my lover and I
grow more than just fonder of one another
it creates only what words can describe as a
feeling of pending doom that will cause one's heart
to break into billions of pieces and all
the supernatural deities of Heaven or the depths of
Hades could not mend the pieces together of
these two shattering hearts.

Even three little words that mean describe the feeling
of I miss you is too menial and a very cheap substitute
for the starved lover that is never nourished since
I do not have my lover near my side, but only
his gracious voice that is the most piercing rhythm
that has vibrated throughout my entire soul
and I hear that sultry tone like a sweet
ghostly echo long after that pleasant call has
faded into the frosty midnight of the inevitable goodbye.

The echoes of my lover's voice is the most beautiful music
that has flooded my heart with an ocean of optimism
that washes away the debris of any past sorrow.

The melody of the music makes my entire being want
to always dance and be forever marry but one day
I will not just remember the echoes of my lover's voice,
for the ancient deserts of the Nile with the mysterious pyramids
are now forming a sand storm in my heart calling me
to fulfill my destiny and aboard the magic carpet to my lover's
enchanted realm and walk hand in hand along the warm coral beaches
and golden cities with my beloved Egyptian Pharaoh.

## *Love is Fading*

Even though we seen all the obstacles ahead that
warned us not to, we refused to see the writing on
the wall and now we weep for what we ignored
because love is fading.

Four months ago our hearts became enraptured
and we rejoiced to the orchestra music which played
our song however, that unison melody will not be heard
because love is fading.

Our passion once flowed like a waterfall in the dews
of a lake that resides in the heart of a fairytale forest
Yet, the waterfall will no longer refresh the thirst of the
animals habiting the forest, for the passion has run dry
like the desert because love is fading.

My ambitions once mirrored your pleasant dreams
So vivid were those ambitions and dreams of us and forever
Now those lucid fantasies are shattered by a crack in the
mirror because love is fading.

The old sparks between you and I use to burn so rapidly
that it would ignite a sea of candles or explode into many
beautiful patterns of color that shower a night sky during
a hot July evening, but our sparks have become ashes and
will never ignite into something glorious for our love will
never be everlasting, but fading into past memories and
like a ghost those memories will forever haunt me.

## *Memories From a Reflection*

Walking along a common London street
his hip attire is a contradiction of what he feels.
Though alone it is hard, around many he conceals.
Her reflection in a coffee shop his eyes meet.

For many years, he has not seen
his plan of a wife to be.
She said she needed space, she had to be free
so her shoulder was never for him to lean.

The questionable nature of it all
made him confused about wanting love
or if there was a way for this problem to solve.
For years, he tried to be strong while standing tall.

As the cool rain suddenly came down
vulnerability came across him once more.
Finding no decision to or not to walk in, his tears bore
finally turning him away with a frown.

# Mini Lighthouse of Comfort

The best purchase I ever made
was three winters ago when the age
of thirty was approaching, and I felt
as though the days of my happy youth
was slowly fading like the emerald leaves
of summer when winter spreads it's cool
breeze across the pale landscape.

Even though the misty fog of winter was
intensifying the chills of worry that
traveled up my spine when realizing
that the next decade of age was going
to create unwanted responsibility and
another ten years of losing beauty, the best
purchase gave me hope during a time of
enormous doubt and that is why I refer to
my purchase of life in front of a mini screen
as my lighthouse of comfort.

Even during the hurricanes and tornados that rip through
the calm seas and scenery of a not so perfect
realm and that make the harsh realization
that surrounds each of us with no escape except
through the magical box that is the mini lighthouse
of comfort that probably you and I both possess.

The mini lighthouse of comfort resides on the
night stand very close to my comfy bed and
if my head becomes filled with heavy thoughts
I do not hesitate to reach for my lighthouse of
comfort to distract and kill off those heavy
monstrous notions that corrode and invade a
peaceful and desired calm.

One of the many fascinating functions
of my lighthouse of comfort is that it
transports my field of vision into a trip to
see the entire world and the people in them without
the hassle of actual travel to many lands.

I can exchange glances and hellos
with the exotic, handsome strangers from what
seems to feel light years away without removing
one fiber of my flesh from the warm, soft cushion
of the bed and the self-centered decor that
brings a sense of safety to my dwelling.
How ironic it is to make acquaintances with the
exotic creatures that populate my mini lighthouse
of comfort, because in the outside realm of my
lighthouse lives the familiar routine with cold aliens
that thrive on misery and bad comings.

Ironic in a way that I cannot feel joy with
the lifelong familiar aliens nor can I feel
joy as the nearing outside realm will rob me
blind of beauty and endless happiness.

Therefore I will keep replicas of my present
state and reserve them in a precious tomb that is
my friend, confidant, my mini lighthouse of comfort.

For these reasons, I have signed away my existence
in the dark, cold outside realm and to forever
dwell in the bright, warm sunshine that is emitted
from my mini lighthouse of comfort.

## *My Chances Lie Beneath a Grave*

Stupidity is nothing more but shame
and a role I have played so many times.

I was a coward, afraid to fall
so I let so many down.

A coward in a way,
I said "No!", to a chance in a lifetime.

An existence of happiness,
why was I so foolish to let it go?

Each day I tell myself
I would have done things different

But these are just words
for they cannot go back in time

And I am forever broken
trying to fall in the past.

If something wondrously
would come my way

I would hope not
to demolish it

but it seems that
my opportunities came long ago

and that is why I say
my chances lie beneath a grave.

Along with the torment
as you can see,

vulnerability, quite often,
comes across me.

I ask not for your sympathy
but maybe I am just

a walking example
of what so many mistakes can bring.

# My Lips are the Colors of a Rainbow

I must admit my costumers have a fetish like no other for colorful, liquid upon my lips very much excites them.

My Monday customer demands the traditional red lip for it reminds him of the mother's blazing hot cheeks as she yelled and slapped him in the face. He gazes at the crimson stained lips while I am bent over with his hands slapping my ass causing my tush to resemble the color of my lips.

My Tuesday customer demands the warm orange lip for it reminds him of the juice that his mother spat in his face. While he stares at the neutral, fruity shade on my lips, he begins to drench my face with a slobbery tongue.

My Wednesday customer demands a bright yellow lip for it reminds him of the sun and how his mother left him to the summer heat many, many years ago. As he fixates his eyes upon the translucent yellow, he spills melted candle wax which scalds my torso.

My Thursday customer demands lips of emerald green for he reminisces about years past when his mother was stingy with money, and the greed left him neglected. After his eyes glued upon the striking color while satisfying an animalistic need, he vanishes without paying.

My Friday customer demands the unusual hue of blue for it brings back memories of almost drowning by his mother's hands in the sapphire ocean. Even though a pretty color, yet unique on the lips, the blue hypnotizes this client to submerge my head under water while he lets loose his carnal desires.

My Saturday customer demands the deep, royal indigo for the royals in this color conjures up royal, painful memories when his classmates taunted him for the flamboyance in the indigo, lace dress that his mother enforced. As my indigo lips transport him to an uneasy and painful place, he tears off my dress and paints my entire body with the colorful past.

My Sunday customer obsesses over a violet lip for the pale purple shade springs to mind his once and only Violet. No not a lover, nor wife, not even a school crush, but his sweet devoted pup that erased the lonesome void caused from his father's absence until a jealous mother took a notion to destroy a beautiful flower and for this the faded purple upon my lips has released an excitable rage that possessed my Sunday client to dismember any good feature I had and tattoo my heart with a rainbow of vengence.

## *Possession*

Unattainable and impossible to reach
you still belong to me.
Even though others will preach
that I do not have what it takes to be in your realm
you still belong to me.
Let them whisper about my fantasy that will lead to sorrow for the
blasphemy of their words will not end my dreams of you tomorrow.
When the daylight breaks you will still belong to me.
How rare and precious that beautiful angelic face it is like
the thrill of coming across an expensive gem among common stone.
There will certainly not be anything to take its place.
You are one in a trillion and still belong to me.
Harmony is the combination of that thick forest of raven hair,
eyes that resemble the ocean so blue, the dimple chiseled upon your chin,
not to forget a porcelain doll complexion that is so smooth and fair.
Describing a sight of perfection is endless and that is you my dear.
Images of you linger in my thoughts, oh how it is driving me mad
and yet you do not even know who I am, how sad.
Despite the fact that this obsession will cost my own sanity
you will forever belong to me.

## Sadie's Leash

Oh, how under control
you look, wearing the black leash
I keep secret in my room.

So submissive, you know
how to turn a girl,
like me, on very well.

Not to be cruel
but only by this
do I feel closer.

When I see you look up at
me on all fours, with eyes
filled with love and adoration

I get a sudden rush
as though I were headed to descend
a steep hill on a rollercoaster.

I bend to pet your
golden hair then your
smooth bare skin.

I use my hands to cuff
your wrists and you
surrender your desires to me.

We tumble to the ground
and I am no longer in control
but smothered in drooling kisses.

Once in a while
you will call out my name
with intense orgasmic pleasure.

The leash still hanging from your neck
makes me wonder, how bizarre, but yet
how great it felt, portraying ownership.

# *The Blue Rose*

In the big garden many beautiful flowers bloomed. However there were two red roses that were greatly admired for being the most beautiful flowers in this floral landscape. They received tons of attention from every kind of flower from the daffodils to the sunflowers. Along with so much attention on their beauty, they had a plethora of suitors. All of this simply for their crimson colored petals. Despite the roaring affection over these two beauties, there was a third rose in the landscape. Now this third rose did not have the crimson color. In fact the petals were blue. For this reason many flowers began to look upon it as if it were a defect, even a mutant. Unlike the warm affection the two red roses constantly received, the blue was taunted daily. Ugly, distasteful, unpleasant, abnormal were just a few of the painful words that the blue rose had to endure. If the other flowers were not shouting emotional persecutions at this rose, then they were simply ignoring its existence. Even the two crimson roses were ashamed that they were a rose just as this freak Mother Nature had cursed. Drenched with relentless sorrow and loneliness the blue rose cried every day. Not realizing the positive effect from the moisture of the teardrops, the rose's sapphire pigment became more intense and the petals rapidly bloomed in number. One day when the gardener was mending to his flowers, he came across the blue rose. To him the rose had an enchanting, alluring beauty compared to the many other beautiful flowers in his garden. The gardener got a wonderful idea for the rose's alluring appearance. He would photograph this creation as if it were an exceptional piece of art. This news came as a sudden shock to the other flowers for the gardener never took photographs of any of them. He never even showered them with as much compliments as that dreadful, ugly, blue monstrosity he called art. With all this news, the floral community got very jealous. They concocted a sinister plan to destroy the gardener's beloved flower. At night when the gardener was asleep they drenched the rose with gasoline. All while they were doing this, the rose cried out for help as it began to sob tears. Unfortunately, the gardener did not hear the rose's cries in time to stop this abominable act. He finally awoke to the smell of smoke. After he looked around his house for signs of a fire, he went to his backyard. In the backyard is where he discovered the horrendous sight of his once beautiful rose set to flames. The long sapphire petals were now ashen and brittle. They fell to the ground in pieces. Just like the scorched pieces to his beloved flower, the tears of the gardener also fell to the ground. His heart was breaking for he no longer had the beautiful muse to photograph.

# *The Everlasting Rose*

What an awesome wonder is it to witness a powerful moment blossom into a memory that can never be shattered.

Moments that made up one's childhood fancies and teenage whims turn into yester years that come to the mind in desperation.

Desperation that the soul shall forever long in time of good and bad.

I knew of a boy of so long ago who brought bundles of joy to my yester years.

Eyes of an enchanted ocean so blue, olive skin with hair the color of night.

The smell of baked apple pie and harmony with great anticipation along with that haunting melody from that warm summer afternoon.

Forever these will remain not in reality, but in memory. Even so throughout one's entire life most everyone you meet will fade away, but underneath this harsh reality lies an honest truth.

This honest truth is these memories shall stay clear and perfect unlike reality.

Maybe for this reason moments grow into memories, because if the moments had an everlasting life they would not survive like that perfect picture in the mind.

They would just grow to be ugly as reality.
For enduring the journey of life almost always brings setbacks and trials.

Thoughts of bliss erases all that hurts causing relief.
For if I am face to face with poverty or become like
an island that is immersed in isolation, eyes turning to
clouds forming raindrops to flood my heart let it nourish
the rose that stands among dead leaves showing how my
memories will always be engraved even though the moments
have passed away.

## *The Harlot*

Why go where matrimony and vows
are the count to everyone's heart
for there you have no reason.

Give up the ghost of yesterday's
dream and come to realize the harsh
reality of street corners and tricks

is what you tell yourself but another
thought provokes of breaking those
habits and then you try even harder

but long lives the
disappointment that seems
hard to break and anger rises.

Slowly you drift back into a
state of acceptance without further
ever looking forward to a different path.

Night by night, you lay down
like a horse with so many telling
yourself to pretend you are somewhere else.

Tell more lies to yourself
to silence the conscience
and wrecked what is self worth.

By morning all that know
are exchanging jokes leaving
a glass filled with shame.

Go seek love my dear, some say but
while still love is missing, even then love can
not wash away the stains of one's notorious past.

## *The Man of Sublime*

In farewell and goodbye oh how
the distance grows in the tie
that bonded one another together.

In reunion how unfamiliar yet in
some way still peculiar, the tie that
once bonded us depends on desire.

Success, when it says now each
and most will instantly bow.

When it tells us to, oblivious
toward our family and friends
the tie most will never defend.

I once knew a man whom, with
hard work finally found the
light of fame and wealth.

In all his glory and this new
environment he cast a shadow
upon his youth and forgot all about
his old friends and his family.
Ashamed he became towards the
so called lame of our feelings, of our status.
When the very last time I
saw this man of sublime, I
realized if I were in his shoes
could I have turned the same way
if distance along with time were
sculptures and people the clay, but
then again I realized it is impossible
for I know in any situation, cold I
can never grow and that is why, to
this day if sublime turns to destitute
and to my door he arrive know that I
won't turn away his needs to deprive.

## *The Pain Taker*

Alone her existence lingers
for no one will never see
but only experience her miraculous gifts.

What she gave up to be apart
of a heavenly wonder was
the delight of this material existence.

When she finds others in pain
she gives herself up in sacrifice like a lamb
with no conniption or regret.

She is full of scars and charity
but charity outweighs self pity
for self pity is only for a fool.

Once she gave herself in the line of fire
for someone she never knew
because the bullet was no threat.

In a case like her
the knowledge of what this person
felt was fear, she could never feel.
On the dark, lonely streets is her usual
home giving hope to the many outcasts.
She shows up in broken families
receiving the unforgettable mark
to relieve the very innocent.

With nowhere to call home,
while many would not give one inch
to take on the burdens of her heavy load

she always seems to survive
on a dream that angel wings
she will someday receive

allowing her to fly beyond
the clouds and into a kingdom
garnished with glory forever.